T0209615

THEATRE OF
RACIAL CONFLICT

THERE IS NO SUCH THING AS BLACK THEATRE

BUNMI POPOOLA

authorHOUSE®

AuthorHouse™
1663 Liberty Drive
Bloomington, IN 47403
www.authorhouse.com
Phone: 1 (800) 839-8640

Published by AuthorHouse 05/07/2020

ISBN: 978-1-7283-6087-4 (sc)
ISBN: 978-1-7283-6086-7 (e)

Print information available on the last page.

Any people depicted in stock imagery provided by Getty Images are models, and such images are being used for illustrative purposes only. Certain stock imagery © Getty Images.

This book is printed on acid-free paper.

Because of the dynamic nature of the Internet, any web addresses or links contained in this book may have changed since publication and may no longer be valid. The views expressed in this work are solely those of the author and do not necessarily reflect the views of the publisher, and the publisher hereby disclaims any responsibility for them.

How can I be free if the tongue that I adopt mirrors a conflicting image of myself?

- A play: *You Know* by Bunmi Popoola, 1985

The original speech was first presented at the Africa Centre in 1988 in London, England, United Kingdom.

CONTENTS

Foreword xi

Acknowledgement xiii

Dedication xv

Preamble xvii

Introduction.. 1

Background... 4

Deculturalisation of Africa 9

Black Theatre 12

Theatre of Racial Conflict...14

Assumptions...18

Consequences.. 20

Language, Object, Action, and Context 23

Author's Reflection.. 29

FOREWORD

Theatre of Racial Conflict

Reading Bunmi Popoola's *Theatre of Racial Conflict* has brought back to me several vivid memories.

One recollection is of an occasion when I was taken with my secondary school classmates to Apapa Club - an elite school club in Lagos, to see a production of Oliver Goldsmith's play - *She stoops to Conquer*.

Performed by an all White ensemble of actors, the play was part of our English Literature syllabus. None of us from the school contingent would have dreamt of describing the presentation as "White Theatre", even though people of Caucascian heritages were part of a very small minority ethnic or racial group in Lagos at that time.

In another example - the film adaptation of Graham Greene's novel *Travels with my Aunt* featured a leading Black American actor, playing the role of Zachary Wordsworth - An African fortune teller, supposedly from Sierra Leone. The actor in question cut a fine figure, but whenever he opened his mouth to speak, I couldn't believe in the character as a real person.

The usage of sweeping terms such as "Black Theatre" in description of the drama of African people and their Diaspora communities often creates situations when the rich diversity of African heritages is overlooked or disregarded at various stages in a production process.

This can be seen in the frequent misleading of roles and the misunderstanding of cultural nuances by directors, critics and audiences alike. Believability in drama is a crucial aspect of its potential to be magical, or truly revelatory.

I have known Bunmi Popoola for several decades. Early shows of his that I saw in London include a stunning presentation of Fugard, Kani and Ntshona's *The Island*. When Bunmi started working in North America, he gave me access to a video recording of his production of Beckett's *Waiting for Godot* which was also highly impressive.

As a fellow theatre maker, I agree with Bunmi about the need for more rigorous thinking and commitment in the creation and appreciation of the drama of Africa and its Diaspora. Some might find the news expressed in *Theatre of Racial Conflict* controversial, but I recommend this text as important reading material for anyone interested in African People's drama.

Juwon Ogungbe
March 2020

ACKNOWLEDGEMENT

I would like to extend my thanks to those actors, actresses, and technicians that I have worked with over the years. In essence they have been my teachers, and in part responsible for my personal growth in theatre. I also want to thank Drama Studio London for the non-doctrinal training that has removed a speck of dust from my eyes, enabling me to see clearly and with a purpose. I would also like to thank Juwon Ogungbe, a *composer, singer* and *theatre maker* who has seen some of my productions over the years and agreed to write a foreword to this work.

DEDICATION

I dedicate this book to both theatre practitioners and theatre going audiences of all races without whom theatre will not exist.

PREAMBLE

Why define a specific genre of theatre as "Black theatre"?

People often make references to English theatre, French theatre, or German theatre, but never Yoruba theatre, Igbo theatre, Zulu theatre, Ashanti theatre and Shona theatre. Instead, African theatres are defined as "Black theatre." Are we subject to an ongoing generalisation by colonialists? And to what end? Is "Black theatre" as a term based on generalisation? Does the term undermine the understanding of Yoruba, Zulu, Shona, or Ashanti theatre? Are these African theatres all the same? If not, why give them a collective term that diminishes their unique identities? Why are they defined any differently from the way European theatres are defined?

If we assume for the purpose of argument that they are the same, then we can safely say that German theatre, French theatre, and English theatre are the same as well, and can be termed "White theatre," based on the assumption that each one of these theatres does not have inherent and unique cultural characteristics of its own.

One of the most reputable journalists in Nigeria, Peter Enahoro wrote in his book *How to be a Nigerian* (The Caxton Press, Ibadan, 1966.):

"Tribes transcend individuality. You would hear one Nigerian describing another Nigerian to a third Nigerian. If the third Nigerian is at sea and does not know to whom his informant is referring, the first Nigerian would then bring him ashore with: "I am talking about that Yoruba man."

In order words, he wouldn't say, "I am talking about that Black man." Indeed, as would Europeans in similar circumstances, you would say, "that German man" or "that French man" and you wouldn't say "that White man" because you want to readily identify whom you are referring to. It would seem that the notion of colour only arises, and all of a sudden becomes important, when Africans and people of African descent are in the same space as Europeans and people of European descent. Europeans and people of European descent feel the urgency to define Africans and people of African descent based on their own agenda, whether they are conscious of it or not.

Those of us who have assimilated the notion that the so-called Black man is inferior to a so-called White man embraced the label with no hesitation, and feel powerless to do anything about it. Some are genuinely not aware that the label is actually obsolete, and that it only exists as a measure of control over Africans and people of African descent by Europeans. This notion is well articulated in Frantz Fanon's book, *Black Skin, White Mask* (Pluto Press, London, 1986). Homi K. Bhabha wrote in his Introduction, (London, 1986), that Fanon asks: "What does a Black man want?" Judging from the contents of Fanon's book and the title of the book, he was really suggesting that a so-called Black man wants what a White man wants; in other words, Black man is forever living in the shadow of a White man. The label is part of his colonial legacy, and we seem to lack the will to shake it off.

The notion of "Black theatre" amounts to nothing more than objectification of Africans and people of African descent's theatres and by so doing making us irrelevant. And it is based on an assumption that by assigning a label to us, we are easy to package, manage, market, manipulate, and control on colonialist terms, or ensure the subjective outlook of colonialism without regard to the inner life of each culture. Alas, we can be whatever they want us to be as we lose our humanity through such references as Black people, Black theatre, Black film, and so on. While our strength and personal growth lies in promoting differences in our theatres, we enabled the colonialists to define our world without any effective resistance and through being indifferent, which in effect has resulted in a series of tragic outcomes such as voluntarily setting our own agenda through colonialist lenses.

Come to think of it, when I was growing up as a child

in the historical small town of Ile-Ife in the Western Region of Nigeria in those days it was rare to see a European. Wherever children gathered and saw a European man, they would shout out, "Oyinbo! Oyinbo!" They were not shouting "okunrin funfun!, okunrin funfun!" which translates as "White man, White man." Making reference to colonialists as "Oyinbo" was not intended as an offence, but as a recognition of difference; Oyinbo is generally used in Yoruba land to refer to Europeans, but does not refer to them as "White men." By so doing they did not negate their humanity, or reduce them to nothingness.

I had a parallel experience as an African teenager in the small town of Lowestoft in the Northeast of England on a working holiday. A group of English children shouted, "Black man! Black man!" in a similar fashion, but no distinctive and human term was applied to me, and my individuality as a member of an African race was dismissed unintentionally by these innocent children because of their social conditioning. I do not perceive my colour as a defining factor in identifying me, so "Why the obsession with my colour?" I recalled questioning myself several years later as I engaged more in inter-racial lived experiences both in theatre and in my day-to-day life.

My conclusion from a series of similar observations is, that whenever Africans or people of African descent come into contact with Europeans or people of European descent they lose their identity or individuality in the relationship because of the imposition of the generalisation "Black." Sadly enough, we the people of Africa and of African descent have come to adopt, internalise, assimilate, and defend this diminishing label to our detriment in an effort to search for our collective identity, which corrupts and obscures our individual identity that was already endowed and vibrant with the cultural identities inherent in us.

INTRODUCTION

I decided to introduce a universal concept to eliminate the gap in perception of the definitions of theatre between races of different colour — *Theatre of Racial conflict* — for the first time when l launched *Elere Yoruba* -Yoruba theatre - with a play based on Barrie Keeffe's play, *Sus,* on August 23, 1988, at the Africa Centre in Covent Garden in London, having finished my training as a theatre director. At that event, I spoke in Yoruba to launch the company, and my delivery was translated by Rosemary DaCosta, a Nigerian actress.

As well documented in so many writings, race by definition is related to biological factors, such as a person's physical characteristics: skin colour, hair, eye colour, and bone structure. The notion of colour as related to race is a hypothetical construct, and there is no such thing as a black skin or a white skin as a category of race. The race doesn't define what we do as artists; what we do as artists is defined through the prism of culture, for instance through Igbo culture, or Yoruba culture and so on because we embody the values, customs, and the traditions of where we were raised. There is no generalised or homogenous colour of Africans and people of African descent, but there are different shades of colour amongst us. There are no races that ought to be called Black or White people. I maintain that this definition is highlighted when the so-called White people want to maintain a comfortable distance from and manipulate the language whichever way they choose.

When I was around 15 or 16 years of age growing up in London, I was particularly always interested in the news of the day, maybe because I was homesick and there was civil war going on in Nigeria when I left the country of my birth. I remember only too well that whenever there was a death in South Africa's B. J. Vorster government, the reporters, who were often of European descent, would always report an African death at the hands of a person of European descent as having been "killed." If it was the other way round the more emotive word "murder" was used. I thereafter referred to the English language as the language of the privileged as demonstrated through all the English colonies. Consequently, I became rebellious and increasingly politicised. It was at that tender age that I started paying attention to the functions of language, and how it could be used to manipulate and obscure the truth. As an adult, my earlier observations reinforced such labeling: when an African and person of African descent is assertive, he is aggressive, when he is confident, he is arrogant. If one is to seek evidence of the reason for classifying people in such blanket terms as "Black" or "White," it lies in the choice of the term used and whom it was meant for. The term "White" was made redundant in a similar context; for instance, there is no such reference made to English theatre or German theatre as "White theatre" in any informal or formal sense. Thus, the application was used to marginalise, misrepresent, stagnate, misunderstand, and make Africans and other people of African descent's theatre irrelevant.

BACKGROUND

In the summer of 1985, I became obsessively preoccupied with the quest for the meaning of "Black theatre." As an upcoming director, I shopped around for somebody or something I could relate to but failed miserably. From then on I realised that I had to find inspiration within myself. The so-called top British Black theatre failed to create an impression on me. In 1984, it became apparent to me that the British funding bodies were having a field day playing political football with the so-called Black theatre companies. What form the politics took is not a matter for this discussion. After seven years of serving my apprenticeship as an artistic director in the wilderness prior to my official training, I came to the conclusion that I could not see how I could practise my craft without defining the term "Black theatre" first, because this would inform my theatrical goals and means of execution.

I was invited to lead a workshop by Harmony theatre in Brixton in which I was preoccupied with the meaning of the word "black" and its relevance to people. At the workshop,

I asked two British born actresses of Caribbean parentage, one Barbadian and the other Jamaican to close their eyes and take the following words in turn, and then say the first words that came to their minds without thinking: Black, Africa, Caribbean.

I took the word black first:

black and then,	**Africa** and finally,	**Caribbean**
Void	Heat	Sunshine
Empty	Trees	Sea
Dark	Nature	Sand
Night	Freedom	Palm tree
Coal	Culture	Holiday
Black people	Dignity	Rum
Death	Sorrow	Sugar Cane
Morbid	Energy	Fruits
Wicked	Sacrifice	Laughter
Mystery	Strength	Awareness
	Beauty	Spiritual
	Black people	Tragedy
		Myth
		Easygoing

I think these words represent an attitude, a feeling that can sometimes constitute an individual's beliefs. Such beliefs, based on a connotative meaning of the word "black" is subjective. For this reason, the word black as applied to a set of people can foster prejudice and racism. Who wants to be associated with something morbid, wicked, empty, or deadly? Prior to doing this workshop I realised that my efforts to define Black theatre was like going on a wild goose chase. I became curious about the relationship between the concept of Black people and deculturalization. I think the use of the former term is a consequence of the latter, given that African ethnic groups are rich with their tapestries of culture.

When I hear someone speak of Black people, I am confused because I do not understand how one can separate a term from its true meaning. A child goes to school, and is told that everything black is evil, wicked, and so on. There is a death in the family, and the members of the family wear all black for the funeral. Just think for a moment of the symbolic significance of black clothes in this context. Then the child is told that he or she is Black or that there is a set of people called Black people. Bearing in mind that no child is born with a concept of the word black or any colour for that matter, how do you propose that such an innocent child should respond to the so-called Black people?

The term is impersonal, general, negative, and inexact in its application as related to a human being and therefore has no function other than to undermine and stagnate an individual it is meant to serve; a human being is a dynamic entity and not static like an inanimate object; no wonder it is easy to objectify and generalise about our world. It is a tactic that our oppressors used day in and day out without any retribution, given that language shapes our perception and understanding of the world. When I asked a friend what he meant by "Black people," his response was simple: "It's a political term." This explanation was not satisfactory, and it suggests to me that his definition is a hypothetical construct, and the political context is often corruptible because it is highly subjective. For what other reason do we give a child a name other than to give him or her a sense of identity or individuality? A name can determine the way a child is addressed, and the way in which he or she responds to the world.

Some people will argue that the word "Black" unites people of African descent and contemporary Africans. This is a fallacy. Where is the evidence of this unity? I'll ask you a question in my language, the Yoruba language: "Se ki a lo jo ni ale yi? Otipe ti mo ti jo?" Do you understand me? No. Let me translate: "Shall we go and dance tonight? It has been a long time since I danced." Let's suppose for a moment that I do not speak English. Where does that leave us? Here I am speaking for men and women of Africa who do not speak English. What is the similarity between Africans and fellow people of African descent, other than the colour of our skins? Unity is both artificial and useless when it is based on coercion; it is coercive when it is imposed. It has to find its way through an individual consciousness and be voluntarily agreed upon otherwise it is futile and lacking in commitment. Our strength lies in acknowledging our differences. Then, mutual respect will follow. When we use the word "Black" we undermine differences. When we use the word "Black" we do not acknowledge a specific culture. It is culture that gives us a sense of identity, unity, and belonging.

DECULTURALISATION OF AFRICA

What is the real consequence of identifying ourselves as Black? The answer is quite simple - deculturalisation of African cultures advancing towards an African American status quo type on the continent. It simply means absence of African culture, replaced by mishmash concepts of alien cultures and ideas incorporated with a residue of local African cultures, which in the final analysis will be passed on as 'modern,' presumably giving it what would be perceived as a progressive outlook by some people.

What are the consequences of not acknowledging differences in ethnicity when we portray ourselves on stage?

Surely a theatre cannot be devoid of differences or a culture; these make a character clear and distinctive; a theatre that is devoid of a culture is an empty theatre. When I hear an African calling himself a Black man instead of an Ashanti man, or Mandinka, or Shona man, I am immediately at a loss regarding how to relate to such a person as he would appear to be following fashion. A Yoruba or an Ashanti man would have no excuse because he should know culturally who he is, whereas a Caribbean or an American of African descent use languages such as English, French, Spanish, or Portuguese, which have no relevance to his roots.

The term Black distracts him from addressing the next crucial question: "Who am I?" This question is crucial because it identifies a living culture from the culturally dead. The question, "Who am I?" confines an individual to an existential concern. This is prevalent in America. One may call it a "scratch record syndrome," repeating the same question, Who am I ? Who am I?, year in and year out.

For example, people of African descendant communities in the Diaspora have changed their cultural identity on several occasions through the last few decades: Negro, Afro-American, Black, and presently African American. So, what is in a name anyway? If there is nothing in a name there would not be no need for all these changes of the name. The motivation to change a name, and search for an accurate and positive identity is governed by the collective social experiences of people of African descent in America. Constant inaccuracy in establishing a suitable identity is due to personal sentiment and lack of objectivity, moving from conceptually based names, Black people, heading towards culturally based identity, African American, but without the benefit of an African language.

Unfortunately, preoccupation with identity questions represents a state of mental imprisonment. It happens when one adopts a constant reactionary and defensive posture, instead of a cultural posture without prejudice. Here, I am of course talking in psychological terms. What one is doing cannot be effective unless the first question, "Who am I?" has been answered honestly and correctly, as "who" informs our "how."

BLACK THEATRE

What is Black theatre? From this point onward I shall employ the term "theatre of racial conflict" as opposed to Black theatre. In doing so, I am not indulging in jargon for jargon's sake, but seeking to raise the level of discussion. I find the term Black theatre inept and meaningless; meaningless because there is no such thing as a theatre that is Black or White for that matter. Meaningless only if we are talking about the denotative meaning of the term "black." Such a theatre would be culturally bankrupt, static, and devoid of soul. Unfortunately an idea has to be consciously imposed on the term for it to be operational. It is for this reason that the term Black is political and open to abuse. The connotative and indexical meanings of the word "black" remains supreme, and the denotative meanings of the word is static, that is to say black is black, and cannot be anything else but black, and cannot be anything else other than evil, dull, dark, death, and so on, as was demonstrated by my workshop years ago.

When I was growing up in England, some English

people would often say, "My best friend is Black," when he or she wanted to protest his or her innocence after being accused of racist actions. The first question that often arises in my mind in those moments is, which "black" is he or she talking about? The notion of Black people being all one, or the same makes me feel that the person doesn't know me, or that the statement is impersonal. It is this type of generalisation that permeates through some societies when it comes to relating to the so-called Black people. This is parallel to what you might get in the so-called Black theatre. The perpetrator naively assumes that this attitude is comforting and reassuring to a so-called Black person like me. I have been to an English dinner where I was a token and accepted African face; in such circumstances, generalised perceptions of my world rules, but of course I would always see through it and challenge such uncomfortable references that are sometimes not intended in the spirit of racism; it is simply that the perpetrators have learned to embody both the generalised and racist language, and also learned the demeanour that gives rise to such utterances.

THEATRE OF RACIAL CONFLICT

This concept has a wider application beyond theatre: *Musical Theatre of Racial Conflict*, *Film of Racial Conflict*, *Photography of Racial Conflict*, *Painting of Racial Conflict*; the term is characterised by having been endowed with narrative and/or conflict. It is in the nature of drama to have a narrative and conflict for it to work. In the final analysis, there is no such thing as a Black theatre, Black musical theatre, or Black film, or Black photography, or Black painting. The definition ought not to be derived from the creator, but from the creation itself, hence the creation speaks for itself. This, in my own humble opinion, is a far more objective way of arriving at the definition. So it is possible for an English person born of African descent to paint a painting that is very English, or to produce a theatre that is English without having to place any emphasis on his or her colour, as colour is devoid of his or her creation having presumably assimilated into English culture and probably having not lived a fully Yoruba, Shona, or Wolof experience in his or her life; so such an individual is likely to produce English theatre, and not Yoruba, Shona, or Wolof theatre.

Have you ever spoken to a so called Black man on the phone who spoke eloquently like an English man or French man only to find that he is of an African descent on seeing him in person; human experience is dynamic, not static, and therefore definition of this activity will be less served by defining it through a person's colour. This is to a large extent suggesting that we are products of our environments, and also inferring that our choices are determined by our culture and not by colour; paying more attention to physical attributes takes us away from the truth of what is in front of us artistically.

But our main focus here is theatre. A theatre of racial conflict is a net result of conflicting interaction between two or more individuals diametrically opposite in race, culture, values, attitudes, and behaviour. The conflict is healthy and inevitable. A theatre of racial conflict is universal in its application; it belongs to the English, French, American, Yoruba, Zulu, or Japanese, and not to the Black man, White man, or Yellow man. It is inevitably political: be it between Irish and English, Yoruba and Hausa, French and German, or American and Peurto Rican. The rule is, wherever you have two or more different cultures interacting, you will have a theatre of racial conflict. However, for a theatre to have meaning, it must be specific in its origin. The origin must be endowed with a language, and language in my own opinion is the basis of culture.

The theatre that exists outside the boundaries of a culture is an empty theatre. Such a theatre can only be based on imitation and a mishmash of alien cultures and ideals. USA, Canada, Cuba, Dominican Republic, Jamaica, and Trinidad have been made out of a synthesis of cultures as a result of migration or forced migration as in the case of people of African descent in America and the Caribbean.

There are two types of theatres of racial conflict: "theatre of *intra-racial* conflict," and "theatre of *inter-racial* conflict." Theatre of *intra-racial* conflict is derived out of a situation experienced by a race, and culturally specific group against the background of its own culture, or an alien culture like the USA or any host country like England, or India. It is homogenous, in that it consists purely of a specific race or group bounded together by a common language. In this case, it doesn't matter whether the language of the host country is used or not. The examples of theatre of *intra-racial* conflict are *The Lion and the Jewel* by Wole Soyinka, *Gods are not to blame* by Ola Rotimi, *Educating Rita* by Willy Russell, *Uncle Vanya* by Anton Chekov, *Who's Afraid of Virginia Woolf?* by Edward Albee, *Waiting for Godot* by Samuel Beckett, however, *Ipi Ntombi* by Bertha Egnos, and *Mary Poppins* by P. L. Travers are examples of musical theatre of *intra-racial* conflict; on the other hand, examples of Film of *intra-racial* conflict are *Carmen Jones* by Oscar Hammerstein II, *Aiye* by Hubert Ogunde, *She's Gotta Have it* by Spike Lee.

A theatre of *inter-racial* conflict on the other hand is a theatre derived out of a situation experienced by two conflicting racial groups or ethnic groups or multiracial groups of varying backgrounds. The group can also include the host. Often the host's language is used, but the language used can be that of any of the individual members of the group: *Death and the King's Horseman* by Wole Soyinka, *Statement* and *The Island* by Athol Fugard, *Sus* by Barrie Keeffe. An example of musical theatre of *inter-racial* conflict is West Side Story by Arthur Laurents.

The notion of Black theatre or White theatre, if it were to be called as such, for that matter cannot be truly defined as a living entity: drama whether in the form of a theatre or a film by its very nature is a living entity. So-called black theatre that occurs in a given space, as defined by the powers that be is reduced to nothingness, and an example of racism due to generalisation and a static entity and an impression of what is meant to be depicted in a space that has no context because it is objectified by virtue of the definition. The gap between what is happening in drama and the term used to describe it is very wide and requires serious scrutiny by the consumers and drama practitioners alike. A theatrical space is a living culture that should only be identified in terms of its source, which is defined through a specific language. After all, the Europeans and Europeans in the diaspora who often set the agenda do not refer to their theatre as a White theatre.

ASSUMPTIONS

When people define the theatre or film that belongs to Africa and people of African descent as Black theatre or Black film, they are suggesting in effect that they are all culturally the same.

For example, Spike Lee's films *Do the Right Thing*, and *Jungle Fever*, are all films of *inter-racial* conflict. This film is defined through the colour, assuming race as a source of conflict, but the conflict arises out of African Americans' unique social circumstances and their interaction with people of European descent. *She's Gotta Have It* is a film of *intra-racial* conflict. Neither of these films has direct relevance to Yoruba or Zulu experiences because they grew out of, and occurred against the background of American culture, which is alien to Yoruba and Zulu cultures. The language and the images and symbols produced on the screen are foreign to Yorubas and Zulus.

The term Black theatre predetermines the perception, goal, and solution to a dramatic problem. The term Black theatre predispose one to ask the wrong question because the term Black theatre is meaningless even if the answer could be right within the context of the question asked. The main body of the term Black theatre or Black film itself is wrong. The essence of Black theatre or Black film does not acknowledge diverse cultures or the individual. It only sees culture and individuals in conceptual and political terms. It fails to recognise that individuality is necessary for cultural growth and a specific cultural reference is compulsory in order to give identity and hence life to a theatre. Non-specific cultural reference produces many bogus experts and opportunists. I am convinced that communicative and effective theatre or film is born out of rigorous human consideration irrespective of the source of inspiration.

Black theatre does not have cultural boundaries, since there is no such thing as a Black language. Therefore what people define as Black culture is loose in its composition and rigid in ideology. This is dangerous not only because of its autocratic nature as it does not invite theatre practitioners to school themselves in culture and the term Black theatre lends itself to racism by way of reference. It also undermines the artistic integrity and creative power of the individual.

CONSEQUENCES

The consequences of labelling a theatre or a film "Black" is deculturalisation. Deculturalisation is essentially a process of depersonalising an individual within a group of people or the entire group sharing a common language. The people of African descent in America have been subjected to what l call mass deculturalisation through slavery. The result of calling a theatre "Black" is that it ensures both maintenance and perpetuation of a deculturalisation process.

Now here is the reason why this subject is the focus of my attention: casting. It seems to me that if we can talk about Black theatre or a Black film, we can equally talk about a Black actress or a Black character. As a theatre director, I have a problem with this mode of defining what I want. For instance, let's suppose that an advertisement is put out for me by my administrator that reads: "A Black actress is required to play a Black character in *The Lion and the Jewel* by Wole Soyinka." This description of what I want amounts to nothing but generalisation. It lacks depth and is disrespectful of the culture I hope to depict in the production. This is so in three respects:

Firstly, it does not tell my readers or listeners about the cultural context of the world which the character inhibits. It should read: "An actress is required to play a Yoruba character called Sidi in *The Lion and the Jewel* by Wole Soyinka." This is more specific, accurate, and respectful. This asks the question of an actress straight away, who is Sidi? What are the characteristics of this character, and so on. Specific cultural reference precedes who.

Secondly, we are not in the business of colour identity, but we are in the business of cultural identity and there is no such thing as a "collective Black culture" that assumes the same identity. This is a pathetic generalisation. It is an illusion in much the same way as the idea of World government is an illusion.

Thirdly, to talk about Black theatre or a Black character is to conceptualise theatre or characterise theatre, paradoxically to an unidentifiable point. A theatre of racial conflict or a film of racial conflict seeks to define performing arts from a humanistic, culturally specific, and universal cultural stance, and not from a generalised conceptual point of view. The secret is to focus on the creation, and not the creator, there lies the truth in the theatre and the arts as a whole.

The difference between people of African descent from America and the Caribbean on the one hand and Africans on the other is simply that the people of African descent have different views of African theatre and arts because they are far removed from the cultural experience that gave rise to their artistic expression. The Africans in Africa naturally acculturated to African theatre and arts because for them it is a living experience. Some people of African descent tend to impose incompatible ideas on African culture, which is already intrinsically buzzing with its own ideas. The Africans in Africa naturally relate to the arts because for them it is a living experience, and not a museum piece. I am not claiming that an African American cannot play an African role which would require serious research for an individual actor to immerse into. When it is badly researched it can come across as a parody of the character, but when the actor embodies the character it is magical. One cannot fully appreciate a culture unless one has lived in it and participated in the living process. Such a pre-condition would involve learning the language and leaving all one's preconceived ideas and views of Africa in the respective countries of origin.

LANGUAGE, OBJECT, ACTION, AND CONTEXT

Black theatre as a concept in lieu of Zulu theatre, Shona theatre, or Igbo theatre implies that there is no consideration for language, object, action, and context relations which are imperative for a culturally specific, communicative theatre; and it is necessary to make distinctions between Yoruba, Zulu, Ashanti, or African American theatres because ultimately our differences do matter and our unique experiences that arose out of those differences matter; it is those differences that will make our potential unity as Africans and Africans in diaspora, when it is realised, formidable and resilient as a unifying force, therefore a generalised idea embedded in black theatre is problematic: the results are disunity, self-alienation, self-hate, and progressive deculturalisation as the Africans and Africans in diaspora continue to emulate European cultures whilst leaving their own cultures behind.

The first issue is that the colonial language we use - English, Portuguese, French, Spanish, and so on insulate us from our own, it is as if we are indulging in self-imposed exile in an open prison, exiled from our own cultures, theatres, and Arts generally. As those languages were enforced in the first place till we eventually developed appetites for them and got lost as our taste buds no longer recognise, or entertain our own languages. To be progressive is to entertain the foreign ways; they do not serve our purpose, or needs, or reflect our inner world, and our unique thought processes are dictated by our languages and cultures. The usage and context do matter.

When considering a theatrical performance, the relationship between language, object, action and context matter without a doubt. When it is generalised as defined by the notion of black people, or black theatre, it invariably obscures the meaning and ultimately results in misinterpretation. For instance, a Language, object, action, and context relation example is as follows: *Stool*, so called in England as a functional object of sitting on is of a particular shape in Yorubaland, it is small and low, up to the top of one's ankles in height, and it is called *apoti* in the Yoruba language, whereas in England, it is under one's waist in height, so sitting on this object is different from culture to culture, hence the object is culturally defined in terms of its form, size, and activities that are performed whilst sitting on them.

Picture a Yoruba woman in a village, sitting on an *apoti* under a tree, peeling an orange; She would have needed to squat to sit. In comparison, an English woman sitting on a *stool* in a bar to have a drink of alcohol would tend to cross her legs or close legs whilst sitting. If they swap roles, getting a Yoruba woman to sit on a stool at the same bar, she is most likely to sit without crossing her legs, but the legs remain apart, whereas if one asks an English woman to sit on apoti, she would have no choice but to sit with her legs apart. This illustrates the relationship between object, action and context, therefore working knowledge of a relevant culture matters in order to perform a given role. Hence the relationship between language, object, action, and context is paramount to create authenticity; the way the language is spoken necessitates that the actors knows he is doing Yoruba theatre and not black theatre in order to engage in the work respectfully in much the same way as German theatre would not be passed off as white theatre in order to implicitly demand certain expectations of actors, for instance, so it is not loosely perceived as a white theatre even though it would never be described as such. Specifically has a tendency to create a mindset psychologically, that matters because it focuses everybody on the task at hand.

There are omnipotent or arrogant mindsets created by this generalised concept of black theatre amongst certain people of African descent in the diaspora, more specifically African American in the USA and Caribbean; there is a notion that they can bluff their way through any African performance simply on the grounds that they are so called black people - most tragic! I had a personal experience of this in San Francisco, I recall in the early nineties, 1992 to be precise, rehearsing *The Island* by Athol Fugard, after a successful run of it in London; unfortunately, the immigration would not allow my South African actor to join us. I recall an American friend of mine suggested I go to Nancy Pelosi's office in San Francisco, and that she would help. I did so, to no avail even though she was willing to help as time was against us. The play was to open in two weeks; out of desperation I cast a talented African American man to play one of the main characters as I was only able to bring in one actor, who is a British citizen. I had to rehearse him in a week to be ready for the opening night; it was tough on each of us. I took him through the rigour of rehearsal, bless him. I remember he asked if he could do press ups in the prison cell scene. I said an interesting suggestion, but no. He looked disappointed. As far as I was concerned, the text was the primary influence on the play's direction, and planting a caricature of American movie ideas into the play, I saw as a distraction. Also, the African language in the text, action, and context doesn't call for that. At one point, he threw the script away in frustration saying, 'I am a bloody good actor.' The other actor that came with me from London had to persuade him to come back onto the set. That was how intense the rehearsal was. Nevertheless, we delivered on the opening night, not up to my standard, but I did get a professional performance.

The way the English woman and the Yoruba woman sit in the contexts cited are culturally determined. It stands to reason that an African American woman is likely to sit the same way as an English woman sits as a result of deculturalisation. The notion of black theatre is meaningless in this context. If I were to stage a Zulu play, I would have to research how a Zulu woman would sit on a similar object, and not assume that she would sit the same way as a Yoruba woman would sit.

AUTHOR'S REFLECTION

After thirty-one years of considering this concept, it's time to reflect on the relevance of the original speech, and having had a chance to ruminate over the idea of "Black theatre" three years earlier when I devised a workshop for the purpose of exploring the meaning of the word "black". The speech was delivered in 1988. At the outset, my own conviction was that the concept of a "theatre of racial conflict" would still be relevant today. It is universal in its relevance, and will continue to be so; all we need to do is change our mindsets.

What I learned from reflecting on the misguided notion of "Black theatre" is that it is not far removed from the same mindset that gives currency to racist concepts; underneath it all lies generalisation of identities in the world that *Other* inhabits. By *Other* I am referring to the so called Black people and folk in similar circumstances, thereby making them subservient to a governing culture, and making the *Other's* cultural identity irrelevant, except when an idea is borrowed from it to enrich the dominant culture by way of osmosis rather like a sponge absorbing water, metaphorically speaking. Every culture has a trait of being semi-permeable; especially in this current Global village.

In 1988, the year of my graduation as a theatre directing student at Drama Studio in London's Ealing Broadway, there was a school anniversary celebration. Many external professional directors, actors, and others who had something to do with the dramatic arts were invited to the Drama Studio London's anniversary celebration. A particular director whom I engaged briefly in conversation stood out in my mind. In the course of our brief discussion, I made a point of proudly saying to him that I was going to direct my countryman's play for my final, Wole Soyinka's *The Lion and the Jewel*, to which he responded boldly, "Who cares about an African play?" I have to admit that my heart sank at that point, and I was embarrassed about even mentioning it. His words echoed in my mind over and over again as though I was rehearsing it for a performance. A few days later, I heard a voice in my head saying: "Who cares indeed?" as though I was agreeing with him. I heard repetitions of the echoes of this question for days as if I had an auditory hallucination even though the source of the question was very real. I came to terms with his way of thinking: "Yes nobody gives a damn, why should they?" He was right. I made it my task to overturn this mindset by identifying a human way of defining our theatre world.

It is that thought that brings me to this speech at the time of delivery. I thought of making a difference by re-appropriating the meaning of theatre without diminishing it to nothingness with the term "Black theatre." I remember directing *Sus* by Barrie Keeffe in 1988, and then in the early '90s directing *The Island* by Athol Fugard, John Kani, and Winston Ntshona. One crucial point is that, comparing so-called Black theatre with often culturally defined English theatre in all the time l have been in theatre, I have never heard anybody refer to British theatre or European theatre as White theatre, but on the contrary, one hears African theatre often referred to as Black theatre. This suggests to me that the so-called Black theatre is irrelevant in the perception of Europeans and people of European descent, and also suggests lack of respect for African inherent cultural characteristics or identities. The people of African descent and some Africans directly from the continent are equally guilty of this phenomenon.

When l was new to San Francisco in 1992, I visited the African Cultural and Historical Society in Fort Mason, San Francisco, California to research the city's theatre scene in San Francisco. A phone call came in unexpectedly from an anonymous Hollywood casting director to the Society to enquire if they knew anybody who could translate a sentence from English into a South African language; I was asked unhesitatingly by the Society's director, on the basis that I am an African. I told her that the only African language I speak is Yoruba from Nigeria; the casting director willing to have me translate the sentence into Yoruba so that they could use it inappropriately and out of context in a film that was set in South Africa as a substitute for a South African language. I refused. In my mind I thought such is the contempt the filmmakers had for African cultures. This was a post-discovery of *theatre of racial conflict* as a concept. I recollected directing *The Island* by Athol Fugard even though I knew nothing about South African culture and the world the characters inhabited having simply received an invitation to direct the play by a London theatre company. I took time out to research the play thoroughly and insisted on being truthful to the text, explored every nuance, including the Afrikaans language in the text, and made sure I cast at least one South African actor in the play who was readily able to contradict any betrayal of the language and cultural expression in the play. Ultimately, listen and hear the voices, the heartbeats, the cries, the laughter, the suffering and jubilation of *Africans* in *African theatre* and not *black people* in *black theatre*. Basically, let the *Africans* speak.

Printed in the United States
By Bookmasters